HORRID HENRY'S SUMMER PUZZLE BOOK

Francesca Simon

Illustrated by Tony Ross

Orion
Children's Books

First published in Great Britain in 2010
by Orion Children's Books
a division of the Orion Publishing Group Ltd
Orion House
5 Upper Saint Martin's Lane
London WC2H 9EA

An Hachette UK Company

The Orion Publishing Group's policy is to use papers
that are natural, renewable and recyclable products and
made from wood grown in sustainable forests. The logging
and manufacturing processes are expected to conform to
the environmental regulations of the country of origin.

ISBN 978 1 4440 0146 4

A catalogue record for this book is
available from the British Library.

Printed in China by Imago

www.horridhenry.co.uk
www.orionbooks.co.uk

HORRID HENRY'S SUMMER PUZZLE BOOK

Francesca Simon spent her childhood on the beach in California, and then went to Yale and Oxford Universities to study medieval history and literature. She now lives in London with her English husband and their son. When she is not writing books she is chasing after her Tibetan Spaniel, Shanti.

Tony Ross is one of Britain's best known illustrators, with many picture books to his name as well as line drawings for many fiction titles. He lives in Oxfordshire.

Also by Francesca Simon

Don't Cook Cinderella
Helping Hercules

and for younger readers

Don't Be Horrid, Henry
Illustrated by Kevin McAleenan

The Topsy-Turvies
Illustrated by Emily Bolam

There is a complete list of **HORRID HENRY**
titles at the end of the book.
HORRID HENRY is also available on audio CD and
digital download, all read by Miranda Richardson.

Visit **HORRID HENRY'S** website at
www.horridhenry.co.uk for competitions,
games, downloads and a monthly newsletter.

HOLIDAY HOWLER

Follow the instructions then read the left over letters from left to right to find the punchline to Henry's howler.

Cross out: 5 Fs, 6 Js, 3 Ks, 7 Ms, 4 Ns, 7 Os, 4 Ps, 5 Qs, 4 Rs, 5 Xs, 6 Ys and 8 Zs

J	M	B	Q	P	E	O	Z	C
R	F	Y	A	X	N	U	K	Z
S	M	J	Z	F	Y	R	Z	E
M	Z	T	Q	O	H	Z	M	J
N	E	X	Z	P	Q	R	S	N
J	K	Y	E	O	X	A	Y	P
W	O	F	Q	M	R	F	O	M
P	Y	E	Z	X	J	K	Y	X
M	J	O	N	E	Q	F	O	D

QUESTION: Why did the crab blush?

ANSWER: __ __ __ __ __ __ __

__ __ __   __ __ __   __ __ __ __

MORE HOLIDAY HOWLERS

*What do you call a man with
a seagull on his head?*
Cliff.

Why is my child so bright?
Because he is my son.

What do you call a cow eating grass?
A lawnmoower.

Why can't cars play football?
They only have one boot.

Doctor, Doctor, I keep seeing insects spinning.
Don't worry. It's just a bug that's
going round.

MY HOLIDAY HOWLERS

Can you write down five hilarious jokes
you've heard this summer?

1. _____

_____

2. _____

_____

3. _____

_____

4. _____

_____

5. _____

_____

PIRATE PRANKS!

Colour in this picture and draw something horrid to fall on Moody Margaret's head — and make her even moodier.

What will you choose?

Goo?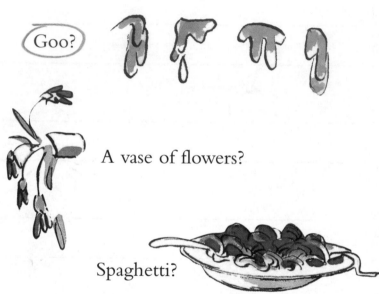

A vase of flowers?

Spaghetti?

 Soggy semolina?

NOTE TO
MOODY MARGARET

CLUB GRUB

Both the Purple Hand and the Secret Club want the hidden store of sweets. But which club wins? Follow Henry and Margaret along the rope to find out.

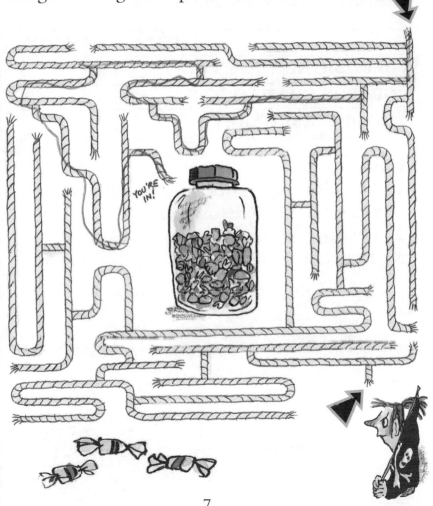

YOU'RE IN!

SWIMMING STARS

Can you work out who is competing in which race, and which medals they won?

RACES: backstroke, crawl, butterfly
MEDALS: gold, silver and bronze

	RACE	POSITION
AEROBIC AL	gold	
GREEDY GRAHAM	bronze	
MOODY MARGARET	silver	

Clues

1. Moody Margaret didn't do as well in her race as Greedy Graham did in his
2. Greedy Graham did the backstroke
3. The person who did the butterfly came first

FOOTBALL FUN

Henry is using all his skills — elbowing, barging, pushing and shoving — to win the game. See if you can spot where the ball should be on these three pictures. Draw an X to mark the spot.

FAMILY MIX-UP

Do you know the names of Horrid Henry's family?
Can you un-muddle the words below and
complete their names?

Write your answers here:

1. PRISSY **YLOPL**   _P O L L Y_
2. RICH AUNT **BYUR**   _R U B Y_
3. PIMPLY **UPAL**   _P A U L_
4. GREAT-AUNT **AETRG**   _G R E T A_
5. VOMITING **RVAE**   _V E R A_
6. STUCK-UP **EETVS**   _S T E V E_

HORRID HENRY NAMES

Can you think up your own Horrid Henry names
for your family and friends? Remember to start
both words with the same letter for every name.

Abomanbe Alex
dinfo dinfe

H WORDS

Can you fit all the H words below into the criss–cross puzzle? Start with the longest word.

3 LETTERS HAM
4 LETTERS HILL
5 LETTERS HELLO, HENRY
6 LETTERS HORRID, HOORAY
7 LETTERS HAMSTER, HOLIDAY
8 LETTERS HOLOGRAM
9 LETTERS HALLOWEEN

SPLIT WORDS

Here are eight six-letter words, but they have all been split in half. Can you solve the clues and put the pairs together?

DER NIC PER NUM BIT
NUT LET MON PEA JUM
RAB SPI KEY PIG BER PIC

A baby pig	PIG	LET
A meal eaten outside, packed in a hamper		
Something you wear when it's cold		
An animal with long ears and a fluffy tail		
A cheeky animal with a long tail		
It can be bought salted or in its shell		
100 is one, and so is 7		
A creepy crawly that spins a web		

MUSEUM MAZE

CLITTER–CLATTER! Horrid Henry
has wrecked the skeleton in the Town Museum,
and the guards are after him. Can you
help Horrid Henry find his way out?

WAY
OUT

MUMMY MUDDLE

Horrid Henry is a menace with the Mummy Kit. Can you untangle the loo roll trail, and discover who he has wrapped up today?

FLUFFY

MUM

PETER

CODE LETTERS

Horrid Henry has written a note to Perfect Peter.
He's used a secret code so that his mum and dad
won't read it and stop him watching TV.
Can you break the code and read the note?

CLUE: If A = Z and Z = A,
can you work out all
the letters in between?

Now use Horrid Henry's code to write your own note to Perfect Peter.

FAVE FOODS CROSSWORD

Fill in the crossword and find out Horrid Henry's favourite foods.

Across

2 Red and squirty – looks like blood!

4 Salty and crunchy. Made from potatoes.

6 Horrid Henry's favourites are Big Boppers and Dirt Balls.

1 BURGER
2 KETCHUP
3 CHIPS
4 CRISPS
5 PIZZA
6 SWeets

Down

1 Round and beefy, and served in buns.

3 Fish and _ _ _ _ _!

5 Big and round, with cheese and tomato on top.

HORRIBLY HEALTHY FOOD

Henry's mum is planning a horribly healthy menu for Horrid Henry's party. To find out the menu fill in the answers on the dotted lines below.

1. Horrid Henry hates this fruit.
   It's green or red, with a core.

   A P P L E   **JUICE**

2. These fruits are green or black and come in bunches.

   g r a p e s

3. A long salad vegetable with dark green skin.

   c u c u m b e r   **SANDWICHES**

4. An orange vegetable.

   c a r r o t   **CAKE**

5. A pale green salad vegetable, eaten with dips.

   _ _ _ _ _ _   **STICKS**

WHAT'S FOR TEA?

Cross out all the letters that appear more than once on Horrid Henry's plate. Then rearrange the letters that are left to find out why he looks so angry.

Write your answer here: _ _ _ _ _

CRAZY COOKS

Solve the clues below and fill in the missing words – they are all things you might find in your kitchen. Then read down the dark column to reveal something horrible cooked up by Horrid Henry and Moody Margaret.

1 S	u	G	a	r
M	i	L	K	
	3 H	O	n	e	y
		4			

1. Add a teaspoon of this to sweeten your tea
2. This comes from cows
3. This is made by bees
4. This comes in different shapes, like spaghetti and macaroni

HAPPY HOLIDAYS

Henry's idea of a good holiday just isn't the same as his mum and dad's. What sort of holiday would suit you? Imagine your dream holiday, and answer these questions.

1. *What do you dream of doing on holiday?*
(a) Going for good long walks in the countryside – whatever the weather.
(b) Swimming in the sea, building sandcastles and enjoying the sunshine.
(c) Sitting on the sofa, eating crisps and watching TV.

2. *What would be your perfect meal?*
(a) Sausages and baked beans cooked over an open fire.
(b) A beach barbecue and a big ice-cream.
(c) Pizza, chips, burgers, crisps, chocolate and sweets.

3. *What would you be wearing on your dream holiday?*
(a) Walking boots, thick socks, waterproof trousers, woolly jumper and an anorak.
(b) Swimming trunks or a bikini.
(c) Pyjamas – it's a holiday!

4. *What would you bring back with you?*

(a) Muddy boots and soggy wet clothes.

(b) A collection of pebbles and shells.

(c) A collection of sweet wrappers and crisp packets.

5. *What are your top three tips for a dream holiday?*

(a) Fresh air, cold showers and quiet.

(b) Sun, sea and sand.

(c) Comfy beds, hot baths and a giant TV with fifty-seven channels.

Answers

Mostly (a)s: Unlike Henry, you like a challenge, and your ideal holiday is a camping trip without any home comforts.

Mostly (b)s: A traditional seaside holiday is your idea of bliss. So pack up your swimming gear, and your bucket and spade, and enjoy a fun-filled beach break.

Mostly (c)s: Just like Horrid Henry, your idea of a perfect holiday would be to spend every day grossing out on pizza, chips, crisps and sweets and watching all your favourite TV programmes.

CAMPSITE MAZE

Horrid Henry and his family travel on the ferry to France, and then drive to the campsite. But which campsite will they arrive at – Horrid Henry's favourite, Lazy Life, or Perfect Peter's choice?

MY DREAM HOLIDAY

Horrid Henry dreams of going on holiday to Lazy
Life Campsite where there is swimming, music
and TV. Draw a picture of your dream holiday here.

HOLIDAY HIGHLIGHTS

Horrid Henry's family, friends, and enemies have special holiday highlights. Untangle the names and work out who enjoyed what.

1. Day out at a theme park **EAATGRMR**
Answer: M a r g a r e t

2. Watching a football match **SMSI ELBTTA-XEA**
Answer: M i s s b a t t l e - a x e

3. Swimming with dolphins **GGSYO DSI**
Answer: __ __ __ __ __ __ __ __

4. Long lie-ins every day **DNLIA**
Answer: L i n d a

5. Trip to an ice cream factory **MGAAHR**
Answer: __ __ __ __ __ __

6. Going on a nature trail **RPTEF**
Answer: P e t e r

7. Attending the Summer School for Clever Kids **NBRAI** and **EALCR**

Answer: __ __ __ __ __
  and __ __ __ __ __

ARE YOU A HORRID HENRY OR A PERFECT PETER?

Are you like Horrid Henry –
or more like Perfect Peter?

1. *What do you do with your pocket money?*
(a) Spend it all on sweets and comics. ✓
(b) Save it up to buy something special.

2. *Is your bedroom…*
(a) A smelly mess covered in sweet wrappers and old comics?
(b) Always neat and clean? ✓

3. *When your parents have guests round to the house, do you…*
(a) Try to spoil their evening by being on your worst behaviour? ✓
(b) Help hand round nibbles and nod politely at everything they say?

4. *If you have nits...*
(a) Do you pass them on to as many people as possible?
(b) You never get nits!

5. *If the queen visited your school, would you...*
(a) Ask her how many TVs she has?
(b) Bow and say hello? You've been practising for weeks.

6. *If your parents asked you to vacuum the living room, would you...*
(a) Leave the vacuum on while you watch TV?
(b) Get to it right away? You need some extra pocket money for that new science book.

Mostly (a)s: You are a Horrid Henry! You're messy, rude, lazy and – horrid!

Mostly (b)s: You are a Perfect Peter. You're neat and nice, polite and – perfect!

WHAT'S IN THE BAG?

Horrid Henry's holiday bag is full of comics and sweets, but can you guess what Perfect Peter has in his?

Across
1. Use this to draw a straight line.
4. You can write or draw with this.
6. Square and white – for blowing your nose.
7. You can borrow this from a library.
8. If you cut your knee, use one of these.

Down
2. You can use this if you make a mistake.
3. Something healthy to eat on the journey.
5. These can add colour to your work.

PERFECT PETER'S PICTURES

Henry has been doodling on Perfect Peter's school photos. Can you spot the pairs?

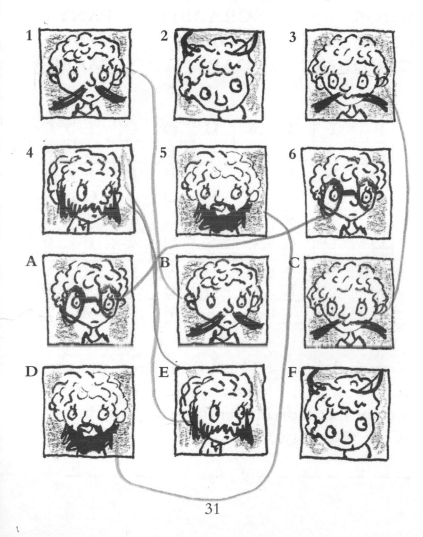

BIRTHDAY PRESENTS

"Ugh!" screams Horrid Henry as he opens his birthday presents. Can you find all the unwanted presents listed below in the wordsearch?

~~BOOK~~   SCRABBLE   PANTS
PENS   GLOBE   VEST
CARDIGAN   SOAP   PAPER

P	P	T	W	H	O	O	E	C
A	A	S	P	E	E	L	A	R
O	N	E	C	U	B	R	S	E
S	T	V	H	B	D	I	O	P
N	S	V	A	I	N	M	J	A
Q	O	R	G	S	N	E	P	P
F	C	A	X	G	L	O	B	E
S	N	K	O	O	B	Z	X	H
R	B	T	S	X	F	X	M	W

Now find the first 14 left over letters and see if you can read the hidden message. It reveals the present that Horrid Henry *really* wanted.
Write your answer here:

_ _ _ _ _ _ _ / _ _ _ _ _ _ _

Now colour in this picture of Horrid Henry dreaming of his favourite presents to take on holiday.

SPORTS DAY

Horrid Henry, Perfect Peter and Moody Margaret each took part in a different race. One of them came 1st, one of them came 2nd and one of them came 3rd. From the clues, work out who competed in which race, and what their position was.

RACES: skipping, sack, egg and spoon

	RACE	POSITION
HORRID HENRY	*bronze*	
PERFECT PETER	*Gold*	*egg race*
MOODY MARGARET	*Silver*	

Clues

1. Horrid Henry didn't do as well in his race as Moody Margaret did in hers.
2. Moody Margaret did the skipping race.
3. The person who did the egg and spoon race came first.

SPORT SEARCH

Can you find all the sports listed below
in the wordsearch?

BADMINTON   GOLF

ROUNDERS

HOCKEY   NETBALL

TENNIS   RUGBY

CRICKET   FOOTBALL

B	T	D	Q	Z	X	E	R	F
P	A	E	D	T	B	O	H	O
F	T	D	N	J	U	X	O	O
C	L	E	M	N	Q	Y	C	T
E	I	O	D	I	I	B	K	B
F	T	E	G	P	N	S	E	A
C	R	I	C	K	E	T	Y	L
S	J	Y	B	G	U	R	O	L
L	L	A	B	T	E	N	X	N

HORRID HENRY'S SPORTS DAY

Write your own Horrid Henry story
about the horrid tricks Henry gets up to
at his school sports day.

_____

_____

_____

_____

_____

_____

_____

_____

_____

_____

_____

_____

Read all about Horrid Henry's Sports Day in *Horrid Henry Gets Rich Quick*

TRICKY TRIANGLES

Miss Battle-Axe has given her class two
puzzles to solve. Can you do them too?

In the first puzzle, move the numbers on to the
rings, so that the total of the numbers on all three
sides of the triangle equals 9.

Numbers
1
2
3
4
5
6

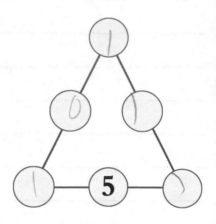

Why not try another?
This time, all the sides have to equal 10.

Numbers
1
2
3
4
5
6

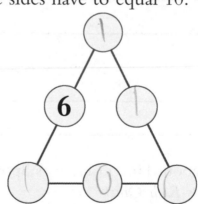

CROSS NUMBERS

Here's a crossword with a difference – it's all numbers! Henry is horrified! So give him a hand with his maths and help him fill it in.

		1		**2**	
3				**4**	**5**
6	**7**			**8**	

Across
1. Number of days in a year
3. 12 x 12
4. Number of days in a fortnight
6. Add 22 to 8 across
8. Number of days in February in a leap year

Down
1. 1 across plus 8 across
2. 499 + 2
3. Add 21 to 3 across
5. 501 – 2
7. Number of players in a football team
8. 7 down x 2

JOIN THE NITS

Moody Margaret's head is crawling with nits. Can you join up the nits and reveal who's holding the scary-looking nit comb?

Write your answer here: _____

PET PUZZLE

Can you find the following pets
in the wordsearch below?

GOLDFISH   HORSE

PARROT   TORTOISE

GUINEA PIG   KITTEN

PUPPY   HAMSTER

MOUSE   RABBIT

E	S	I	O	T	R	O	T	G
G	F	H	A	H	Y	N	I	K
R	O	G	A	P	O	P	J	I
A	H	L	P	M	A	R	P	T
B	E	U	D	E	S	A	S	T
B	P	S	N	F	R	T	S	E
I	Y	I	U	R	I	H	E	N
T	U	X	O	O	B	S	O	R
G	N	T	Z	Q	M	S	H	X

CLASSMATE CROSSWORD

Can you fill in the crossword with the names of some of Horrid Henry's classmates?

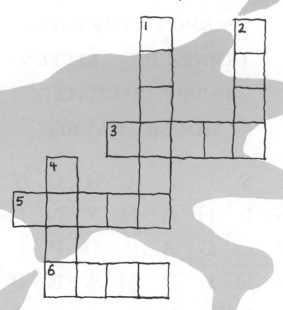

Across

3. _ _ _ _ _ BERT (Biggest boy in the class)
5. _ _ _ _ _ JOSH (Always happy)
6. _ _ _ _ RALPH (Never says please or thank you!)

Down

1. _ _ _ _ _ _ GRAHAM (Eats lots of sweets)
2. _ _ _ _ LINDA (Does as little as possible)
4. _ _ _ _ SUSAN (Like a lemon!)

WEEPY WILLIAM'S DISAPPOINTING DISGUISE

These six pictures of Weepy William on Hallowe'en all look the same. Can you spot the odd one out?

1

2

3

4

5

6

SANDWICHES

Put one letter in the dark column that will finish the first word and begin the second word. For example, S could be placed between BU and MILE to make BUS and SMILE.

BU	S	MILE
CA	t	RAIN
YET	i	GLOO
FU	n	APPY
BOO	k	ITE
CLU	b	ALL
YOY	o	VAL
PLU	m	USIC
WE	b	OOT

When you've finished, the blue column spells out something that will make Horrid Henry smile!

Answer: _S_ _t_ _i_ _n_ _k_ _b_ _o_ _m_ _b_

PICTURE PAIRS

Perfect Peter does a lovely picture of their ferry to France, until Henry doodles on it. There are three pairs of pictures below – can you find them?

A

B

D

C

E

F

ANSWER:
The three pairs are: _____ _____ _____

CAR GAMES

Look out of the car window and see if you can spot something beginning with every letter of Horrid Henry's name? Write your answers here when you do.

H_____

O_____

R_____

R_____

I_____

D_____

H_____

E_____

N_____

R_____

Y_____

Now see if you can spot all of the things on Horrid Henry's list. Tick them off when you see them.

☐ **6** red cars

☐ **4** blue cars

☐ A motorbike

☐ A dog in the back of a car

☐ Somewhere that sells burgers

☐ A registration plate with an H in it

☐ A field of sheep

TOP SECRET JOKES

Some of Horrid Henry's jokes are so rude, he has to write the answers in his top secret code. Can you understand what Henry has written?

What did the constipated mathematician do?

Tuo ti dekrow dna licnep a tog eh.

If you're American when you go into the toilet and American when you come out of the toilet, what are you when you're in the toilet?

NaeporuE,

What jumps out from behind a snowdrift and shows you his bottom?

Namwons elbani-mub-a eht.

HENRY'S HORRIBLY HARD WORDSEARCH

Can you find the list of horribly hard words
below in the wordsearch?

BATTLEAXE   HIEROGLYPHS

CANNIBALS   LAZORZAP

DIARRHOEA

TERMINATOR

FANGMANGLER

TRAPEZIUM

F	S	A	T	N	V	B	N	L	B	J
A	H	K	E	D	C	P	G	A	D	U
N	P	X	R	O	L	Q	T	Z	G	R
G	Y	S	M	G	H	T	I	O	U	O
M	L	H	I	S	L	R	K	R	P	S
A	G	A	N	E	D	C	R	Z	N	U
N	O	C	A	N	N	I	B	A	L	S
G	R	X	T	J	W	F	G	P	I	Z
L	E	G	O	I	L	S	E	U	M	D
E	I	L	R	R	I	M	H	R	C	I
R	H	M	U	I	Z	E	P	A	R	T

WHAT'S IN THE BOX?

Cross out all the letters that appear more than three times on Horrid Henry's box. Then rearrange the five letters that are left to find out what's inside.

Write your answer here:  _ _ _ _ _ KIT

JOIN THE DOTS

"It's as long as my leg," said Moody Margaret. Join the dots to find out what Moody Margaret is talking about, and why Horrid Henry is looking so scared.

Write your answer here: _____

CODE CRACKING

When Greasy Greta, the demon dinner lady, starts pinching all the tasty treats from Horrid Henry's lunch, it's time for revenge.

Crack the code and discover his plan.

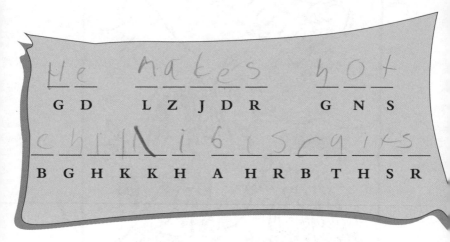

He makes hot
G D   L Z J D R   G N S

chillibiscaits
B G H K K H   A H R B T H S R

CODE CRACKING CLUE:
Replace every letter here with the next letter from the alphabet.

SEASIDE SUDOKUS

Can you solve these seaside sudokus?
Every coloured box must contain one shell,
one starfish, one sun and one ice cream.

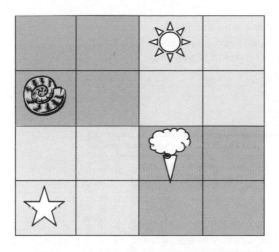

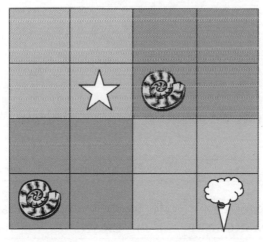

ANSWERS

p1
BECAUSE THE SEA WEED

p.6
Margaret, you Worm.
Watch out!
The Purple Hand is on the attack.
We will steal your biscuits and your dagger.
NAH NAH NEE NAH NAH.
Horrid Henry.

p.7

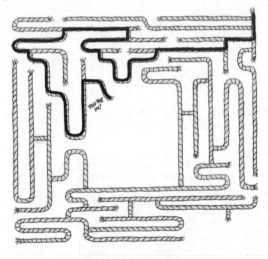

The Purple Hand Club wins.

p.8

	RACE	POSITION
AEROBIC AL	BUTTERFLY	GOLD
GREEDY GRAHAM	BACKSTROKE	SILVER
MOODY MARGARET	CRAWL	BRONZE

p.9

p.10

1. Prissy Polly, 2. Rich Aunt Ruby, 3. Pimply Paul
4. Great-Aunt Greta, 5. Vomiting Vera, 6. Stuck-Up Steve

p.12

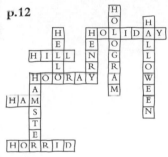

p.13

PIC-NIC, JUM-PER, RAB-BIT, MON-KEY
PEA-NUT, NUM-BER, SPI-DER

p.14

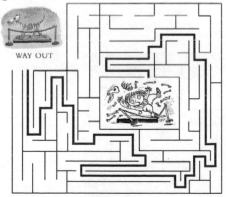

p.15
Horrid Henry has wrapped up Fluffy today

p.16
PETER IS SMELLY

p.18
1 down – Burgers
2 across - Ketchup
3 down – Chips
4 across - Crisps
5 down - Pizza
6 across - Sweets

p.19
APPLE juice, GRAPES, CUCUMBER sandwiches
CARROT sticks, CELERY sticks

p.20
Horrid Henry doesn't like his PEAS

p.21

S	U	G	A	R	
M	I	L	K		
	H	O	N	E	Y
		P	A	S	T	A

Horrid Henry and Moody Margaret cooked up GLOP.

p.24–25

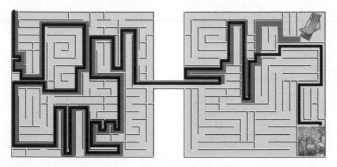

56

p.27

1. MARGARET, 2. MISS BATTLE-AXE, 3. SOGGY SID
4. LINDA, 5. GRAHAM, 6. PETER, 7. BRIAN and CLARE

p.30

1 across - Ruler, 2 down - Rubber,
3 down - Apple, 4 across - Pencil,
5 down - Crayons, 6 across - Hankie,
7 across - Book, 8 across - Plaster

p.31

1-B, 2-F, 3-C, 4-E, 5-D, 6-A

p.32

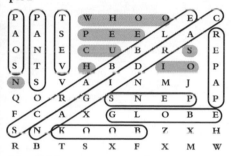

The hidden message is: WHOOPEE CUSHION

p.34

	RACE	POSITION
HORRID HENRY	SACK	3RD
PERFECT PETER	EGG AND SPOON	1ST
MOODY MARGARET	SKIPPING	2ND

p.35

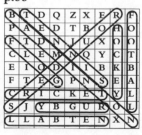

p.38

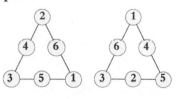

p39

		3	6	5	
		9		0	
1	4	4		1	4
6					9
5	1			2	9
	1			2	

p.40

Nitty Nora, the nit nurse

p.41

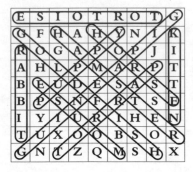

p.42

1 down - Greedy, 2 down - Lazy, 3 across - Beefy
4 down - Sour, 5 across - Jolly, 6 across – Rude

p.43

The odd one out is number 4. Weepy William's ear is missing

p.44

STINKBOMB

p.45

The pairs are A and C, D and F, B and E

p.48

Read backwards

p.49

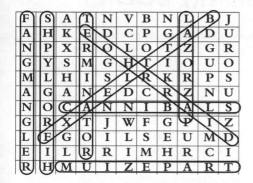

```
F  S  A  T  N  V  B  N  L  B  J
A  H  K  E  D  C  P  G  A  D  U
N  P  X  R  O  L  O  T  Z  G  R
G  Y  S  M  G  H  T  I  O  U  O
M  L  H  I  S  I  R  K  R  P  S
A  G  A  N  E  D  C  R  Z  N  U
N  O  C  A  N  N  I  B  A  L  S
G  R  X  T  J  W  F  G  P  I  Z
L  E  G  O  I  L  S  E  U  M  D
E  I  L  R  R  I  M  H  R  C  I
R  H  M  U  I  Z  E  P  A  R  T
```

p.50
MUMMY KIT

p.51
It's a NEEDLE

p.52
HE MAKES HOT CHILLI BISCUITS

p.53

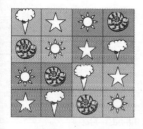 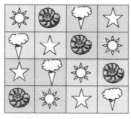

HORRID HENRY BOOKS

Horrid Henry
Horrid Henry and the Secret Club
Horrid Henry Tricks the Tooth Fairy
Horrid Henry's Nits
Horrid Henry Gets Rich Quick
Horrid Henry's Haunted House
Horrid Henry and the Mummy's Curse
Horrid Henry's Revenge
Horrid Henry and the
  Bogey Babysitter
Horrid Henry's Stinkbomb

Horrid Henry's Underpants
Horrid Henry Meets the Queen
Horrid Henry and the Mega-Mean Time
  Machine
Horrid Henry and the Football Fiend
Horrid Henry's Christmas Cracker
Horrid Henry's Christmas Cracker
Horrid Henry and the Abominable
  Snowman
Horrid Henry Robs the Bank
Horrid Henry Wakes the Dead

Colour Books

Horrid Henry's Big Bad Book
Horrid Henry's Wicked Ways
Horrid Henry's Evil Enemies

Horrid Henry Rules the World
Horrid Henry's House of Horrors
Horrid Henry's Dreadful Deeds

Joke Books

Horrid Henry's Joke Book
Horrid Henry's Jolly Joke Book

Horrid Henry's Might Joke Book
Horrid Henry versus Moody Margaret

Activity Books

Horrid Henry's Brainbusters
Horrid Henry's Headscratchers
Horrid Henry's Mindbenders
Horrid Henry's Colouring Book
Horrid Henry's Puzzle Book
Horrid Henry's Sticker Book

Horrid Henry Runs Riot
Horrid Henry's Classroom Chaos
Horrid Henry's Holiday Havoc
Horrid Henry's Wicked Wordsearches
Horrid Henry's Mad Mazes
Horrid Henry's Crazy Crosswords

Early Readers

Don't be Horrid Henry
Horrid Henry's Birthday Party
Horrid Henry's Holiday

Horrid Henry's Underpants
Horrid Henry Gets Rich Quick
Horrid Henry and the Football Fiend